SARAH,

EMBRACE CHANGE!

Cheryl

Change is on the Wind

Managing Change for a New Landscape

Cheryl P. Duvall

with illustrations by

Caroline Devereaux

A Maple Creek Media Publication
Hampstead ◊ Maryland ◊ USA

Copyright © 2014 by Cheryl P. Duvall

Printed in the United States of America

ISBN-13: 9780991244294
ISBN-10: 099124429X

Cover art and interior illustrations created by Caroline Devereaux

MAPLE CREEK MEDIA

P.O. Box 624
Hampstead, MD 21074
Toll-Free Phone: 1-877-866-8820
Toll-Free Fax: 1-877-778-3756
Email: info@maplecreekmedia.com
Website: www.maplecreekmedia.com

Praise for

Change is on the Wind

"You can't become what you need to be without change. Cheryl has taken her years of experience, cast them as an entertaining fable, and given us a charming way for any organization to think about and manage change." ~ **Don Goeman, Executive Vice President, Research, Design, & Development, Herman Miller, Inc.**

"Responding to the realities of competitive markets and shrinking real estate, 'Change is on the Wind' provides a simple roadmap for managing change in challenging times. I especially related to the pilot project. Don't overlook that step if you want to ensure complete success." ~ **Victor M. Polanco, Managing Director, True Partners Consulting LLC**

"This adventure of change, team work, and leadership will move your herd!" ~ **Bonnie Cauthorn, IIDA, ASID, Principal, Design Source Inc.**

"*Lions and tigers and bears, oh my! A wonderful, easy to understand, yet thorough treatment of the why, how, and what of Change Management. Each of us can identify with one or more of the characters in Cheryl's story. I roar my approval!*" ~ **John H. Vivadelli, CEO, AgilQuest Corporation**

"*This was a stroll down memory lane as I relived our Renovation 360 change management process. It certainly prepared our staff for our bold cultural changes, and in fact, I think I recognize some of those characters!*" ~ **Jessica Feldmark, Chief of Staff, Howard County Government**

"*In this clever tale, Cheryl takes us through a playful but very poignant journey about workplace change and transformation. She not only shares change management best practices but allows us to experience how powerful the process can be when we harness the collective spirit of an organization. 'Change is on the Wind' is a fun, informative, and non-threatening way to help any organization understand the power of place, and gives the encouragement to boldly step into a new way of working.*" ~ **Kate North, Vice President, e-Work.com and Global Chair, IFMA's Workplace Evolutionaries (WE)**

"'Making the unfamiliar, familiar' is a timeless tenet of fables, learning, and change management. Cheryl Duvall, FIIDA, deftly combines all three in 'Change is on the Wind', to tell the story of a Kingdom (recognizable to all readers) that needs to embrace and enact change. Whether you are considering change for yourself or your organization, or a seasoned expert charged with implementing change, this instructional guide told as a simple fable is an excellent tool." ~ **Cheryl Durst, HON. FIIDA, LEED AP, Executive Vice President and CEO, International Interior Design Association**

"After years of honing her process, Cheryl is sharing her change management methodology through a simple story that the inner child in each of us can identify with. What a clever approach! Perhaps more design professionals will implement change management programs with this as their guide." ~ **Alex Kramer, Principal Officer, Arris, a Design Studio**

"This engaging fable is a powerful tool for design professionals to understand and apply the process of change management with their clients. Discipline-specific jargon is explained and critical actions are sequenced to enable unique opportunities through an evidence-based approach." ~ **Caren S. Martin, PhD, CID, FASID, IFMA, Principal, Martin & Guerin Design Research, LLC, and Associate Professor, Interior Design, College of Design, University of Minnesota**

Dedication

To my husband Dudley Whitney, my amazing partner in business and in life. Thank you for joining me in the journey of change management, for our customers as well as for ourselves.

And to our adult children, Jean-Luc, Philippe, and Kathryn. You prepared your parents well for the ever-changing landscape of life, and we continue to be enriched through your adventuresome spirits and abiding energies.

Preface

In January 2014, I sat down in my office to write a conference proceedings paper required of all speakers presenting at the International Facility Management Association (IFMA) Facility Fusion Conference to be held in Washington D.C. that spring. I'm a commercial interior designer and workplace strategist, and have a passion for implementing change management programs that parallel the design and construction process. This conference represented an important opportunity to share my expertise about leading change programs to help office workers who often have extreme change thrust upon them. Change Management is a growing need in our ever-evolving landscape of workplace design.

I opened my laptop, consulted a few of my previous articles on change management, and began to type. I wrote one paragraph, and then stopped. It just didn't feel right.

Boring. That's all I could think. Boring.

Feeling the need for inspiration, I stood in front of my personal library of business books. A confessed bookaholic, I had many colorful spines on my shelves to peruse. My eyes fell on one old favorite: *Storytelling in Organizations*, by John Seely Brown, Stephen Denning, Katalina Groh, and Laurence Prusak. Picking it up, I thumbed through the pages and noted a few highlighted portions. The next thing I knew, I was comfortably sitting in my Eames chair and ottoman, rereading this book from cover to cover, placing yellow stickies on the pages and writing in the margins. By the end of the book, I knew I wanted to tell a compelling story about change management. And it would begin as a conference proceedings paper.

After exploring several story ideas, I settled on a fable, which then required research on animals and reasonable analogies to workplace design challenges. Due to page limitations for the proceedings paper, the fable stopped at Part One of what I envisioned would eventually become a three-part fable. The impetus to finish the fable arrived when I was selected to reprise the topic of Change Management at IFMA's World Workplace conference later in the year. I could think of no better reason to finish writing the fable that had lived in my head for several months.

This book is written for those who are seeking effective strategies during times of bold change. If you are a corporate executive, facility manager, real estate advisor, interior designer, architect, urban planner, human resource director, organization development practitioner, or program manager, you will recognize many familiar challenges, opportunities, and characters in this fable. You may be surprised at the lessons that are disguised in this storytelling method, and it is my hope that you will pick up on the subtle as well as obvious teachings.

This fable might just be an effective way to convince others in your organization that change management is not an optional program, but a necessary process to achieve ultimate success, resulting in optimal performance, employee engagement, and well-being for all.

Foreword

This fable is an attractive and instructive metaphor for a well-managed relocation by a large organization to a new facility. Cheryl highlights all the critical tasks for a successful move. She also enhances current wisdom regarding change management in two important ways.

First, she dramatizes the fact that, for an organization, the process of planning and implementing a physical relocation is profoundly social as well as technical. Top leadership needs to explore possibilities and embrace opportunities in the new setting while gracefully letting go of what is currently cherished in the old in order for the transition to be a success.

Second, through amusing descriptions of animal characters, she reveals the critical importance of seeking people with a wide variety of skills and abilities to manage the relocation, of working adaptively with their diverse personal styles while making the most out of their strengths, and of orchestrating the process in ways that promote mutual support and team spirit.

This book will serve as an excellent springboard in initial planning meetings for any relocation, as well as provide a helpful reference point as a move progresses.

Eric H. Neilsen
Professor Emeritus, Department of Organizational Behavior,
Weatherhead School of Management, Case Western Reserve University

Introduction

One of the most effective ways to share complex knowledge is to tell a story and allow the reader to make connections to their own reality. As Stephen Denning postulated in *Storytelling in Organizations*[1], "With a story, listeners get inside the idea. They live the idea. They feel the idea... They experience the story as if they had lived it themselves. In the process, the story, and the idea that resides inside it, can become theirs."

Part One

News of the Change

The savanna was changing. King Lion could sense it on the wind many months before he sent scouts to explore the edges and beyond. What they reported upon their return was heart-stopping, but, being the King, he kept a stern poker face and thanked them for their diligence. He knew he didn't have to ask them to stay quiet. They were loyal subjects and were grateful for the honor he bestowed on them.

After they left he pulled an ancient map from beneath his throne. Varying colors showed locations of shrinking forests, grasslands, and ridges that once defined his kingdom. Many seasons before, his domain extended all the way to the sea. But competing kingdoms had claimed the outer edges of his land, burning vegetation to make way for profitable crops and housing, leaving just the eastern edge beyond the Great Divide for possible relocation.

The King sighed. He knew about the region east of the Great Divide. His grandmother had been born there, but forced to leave with the raging fires that ravaged the land during her teens. When the King was still a cub, she had taken him on the long journey to her childhood grounds. The land had fully recovered but was so very different than anything he had ever experienced. The King remembered his grandmother's misty eyes and how her soft voice caught with emotion as she described the unique culture of transparency and collaboration that were the unexpected byproducts of tight boundaries and limited resources. She reminisced about the knowledge and wisdom that was passed seamlessly throughout the community, leading to greater engagement, performance, and wellbeing for each member, young and old.

The King folded his map and sat in silence, pondering the reflections of his grandmother. Abruptly, his mind returned to the scouting report. He could not deny the sense of urgency that was upon his kingdom. If they were to survive, they would have to relocate across the Great Divide, and occupy a land vastly different than their prized savanna.

King Lion drew near the edge of his lair and, looking down, considered how his subjects now lived. Most of the kingdom enjoyed enclosed personal space, like the jackals in their dens and the hawks in their nests. Their spaces were large, with room for gathering resources or simply spreading their wings. They weren't accustomed to sharing lairs or even their tree limbs. But the region beyond the Great Divide would not allow for such luxuries.

Resolved, the King summoned the leaders from the three provinces. Each had differing leadership qualities, and the King valued the breadth of counsel that the three confidants provided. Together, they would help him outline a plan for relocating their kingdom.

First to arrive was Dowager Ostrich of the O Province. The Dowager was aging, but her heavy body was well-supported by her still-powerful legs.

As the Dowager curtsied and exchanged warm greetings, she was almost toppled by the ever-aggressive Lord Badger. Lord Badger tended to act independently, and could always be counted on for an opinion, a quality that the King had grown to admire since it spared the King from becoming mired in the senseless details of the B Province.

As the Badger straightened from his bow, all heads turned as Lady Kangaroo hopped gracefully into the room. Lady K was known to be cool in a crisis and was considered to be a creative problem-solver. She regarded challenges as opportunities for innovation and camaraderie, and could be counted on to "think outside the pouch." She flashed a warm smile as she curtsied to the King.

"Thank you for coming on such short notice," began the King. "I have news to report, and it may shake you to your beaks and paws." He gestured for them to join him on his rock terrace, overlooking the expanse of the kingdom on this sunny and cloudless day.

As they settled, the King partially unfolded the ancient map before them, orienting it to align with the view below. "Two years ago," he began, "I sensed danger to our Kingdom as we know it. I did not want to overreact, yet the signs continued. Exactly one year ago, I sent scouting parties of our finest field mice to investigate. This morning, they returned with a full report of our diminishing land and resources."

The King pointed to the map as he revealed highlights from the scouting report. "As you can see, the land is being encroached from the north, west and south with increasing intensity. This concurs with the complaints we've been receiving from each of your provinces. We now realize our time in this land is quite limited." The King paused, and then stated with conviction, "In my estimation, we have just six months to relocate."

The three advisors sat in stunned silence.

The King was very aware of his leadership responsibilities in this dire moment. "We are not without hope. Our scouts have identified a new home for us. The good news is that land is available, and protected on all sides. It has adequate resources, water, food, and shelter. The bad news is...." The King's voice drifted as he hesitated, and then continued. "It would be better to say that there are two significant challenges to this land. First, it is located across the Great Divide. Second, this protected land is significantly smaller than our current savanna."

"How much smaller?" Lady K inquired, with hesitation. The King met her eyes. He reached for the map and unfolded it completely to reveal the region east of the Great Divide.

The Dowager fell to her side and appeared to bury her head, as ostriches are rumored to do. Lord Badger grunted, his nose flaring while his ears seemed to emit steams of protest. Lady K, although taken aback, began to notice features on the map beyond the boundaries. "Well I can see that this land is MUCH smaller than our kingdom," she said. It may not even be as big as our largest province." Lady K pointed, "But it appears that this land has features that our savanna does not. Is this a waterfall, leading to a lake? What is this open range, and are those wildflowers that border it? What do we *really* know about this region, east of the Great Divide?"

The King was grateful for her astute questions, and shared the stories of his grandmother. Lady K nodded her head, and began to dream the possibilities. Lord Badger calmed down, as he eyed a piece of land that he thought he might acquire for himself. The Dowager lifted her head enough to see a patch of wildflowers that would provide a variety of nourishment she hadn't experienced since her infancy.

23

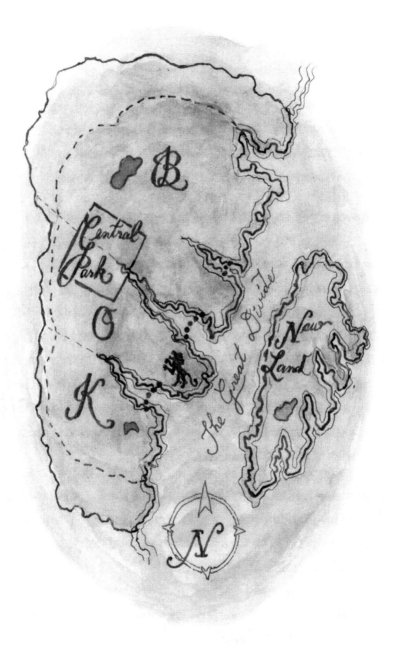

Continuing, the King felt it was important to emphasize the tight space. "Be aware that this move will result in Bold Cultural Change. We must consider how we will handle the loss of enclosed personal space and the reduced size of individual spaces. Be aware that some may not occupy permanent habitats. This new terrain is more open and transparent. Our New Land cannot provide the luxury of our past abundant space. Let's be clear about that!"

The King thought it best to state the obvious: "We must make a relocation plan. In it we must note the major steps, what it will cost us, what it will require of us. We must be very clear about what must be done. I will call a Savanna Hall Meeting in the morning and I will announce to the Kingdom that we are moving in six months, before the rains come. I am holding each of you responsible for the success of our move. You must place a relocation plan for your province before my throne within the week."

The three provincial leaders nodded in agreement. The King rose. The meeting was over.

As the three advisors returned to their provinces with the setting sun, their minds were overwhelmed with jumbled thoughts and concerns. True to their personalities, the actions they took prior to the Savanna Hall Meeting were quite telling. The Dowager went to bed immediately upon her return, pretending that nothing had changed. Lord Badger loudly boasted to his friends that the King had summoned him for counsel due to a crisis facing the Kingdom. He even dropped elusive hints about "impending moves" which began rumors that swept like wildfire across the B Province and into the other provinces by dawn. As for Lady K, she needed to clear her head, so she went for a swim in her province's shallow lake. After putting her little ones to bed, she sat at her desk and began to write a plan. In the middle of the night she had a revelation: they would need not only a plan for moving; they would need a plan for how to live and work in the new land!

~~~~~~~~~~~

The sun rose bright and hot the next morning as the savanna's mighty and small made their way to the Plaza in Kings Park. They were abuzz with speculation, fueled wildly by the rumors from B Province. Margaret "Maggie" Magpie, the King's Communications Advisor, almost crashed into the ground during her flight towards the Plaza, startled by the snippets of conversations she heard from the travelers below.

"Did you hear we are being attacked by The Human Kingdom on the West? They've already decimated half of O Province!"...

"The King summoned Lord Badger to put him in charge of the Kingdom while the King goes away for six months!"...

"We jackals are being made to share our dens with those pitiful winged creatures! It must be the work of those sly foxes, who of course get to keep their private dens! No fair! "

Maggie Magpie wondered why she had been kept in the dark. She chirped to herself, "How can I possibly lead communications when the King won't confide in me?!"

Along the paths below, Hal the Honeybee worried as he flitted from flower to flower on his way to the Plaza. Like Maggie, he could overhear crowd snippets, and he knew that the rumor mill had never been busier, which meant that productivity would hit record lows. As Director of Animal Resources and Operations, he buzzed to himself, "These rumors are sapping the energy out of our workers. No one can focus on their real jobs!"

Finally the whole Kingdom had gathered in the Plaza, occupying every available tree limb, flower petal, sandy patch, and lily pad. When the sun moved directly overhead, King Lion appeared on his high rock terrace, joined by the Dowager, Lord Badger, and Lady K. A hush fell as His Highness addressed the crowds.

"Yesterday, I received news from reliable sources that our land is being threatened on three sides. Our Kingdom cannot continue as we know it. We must move, and quickly. In six months, before the rains, we will relocate." He paused, as cries emanated from the crowd below. He continued, "For now, please understand that all of you must make plans to move. No one may remain here. I have delegated our relocation strategy to each of our three Province Leaders. We will tell you more next week. That is all for now."

With that, the King whipped his tail around and returned to his lair, ignoring questions from the press and shouts from the crowds. Maggie Magpie, in spite of being angry with the King for having excluded her yesterday, flew to her senses and perched on the rock terrace. Summoning her best joyous expression, she tweeted, "Now you heard the King. We will tell you more next week. Now it's time to return home."

Grumbling, the crowd began to leave, but speculations were flying more wildly than earlier that morning. Hal the Honeybee caught up with Maggie, joining the three provincial leaders as they remained on the terrace in hopes of avoiding the questions that were waiting for them below.

Hal blurted, "What the honey is going on?! Are any of you aware that productivity has dropped to an all-time low in just twelve hours?! And that...that...that speech only added more fuel to the fire!" With horrified eyes, the Dowager whispered, "Shhh, that sounds like treason!"

Lady K quickly motioned to move down the terrace, away from the King's ears. Although she wasn't completely prepared to share her thoughts, she took a deep breath and began. "Last night, I sat at my desk until the wee hours of the morning and began to outline a relocation plan for my Province. And the more

I worked, the more I realized that we need more than a relocation plan. In some ways, the move itself is not the biggest challenge. Sure it will be hard, but that's not where the real work is needed."

Lord Badger look perplexed. Dowager Ostrich wanted to bury her head again. Hal and Maggie, who still didn't know all the details as yet, looked like they were about to burst with so many unanswered questions.

Lady K continued. "The real beastly work lies in getting our Kingdom to accept the ways we will have to change to live successfully and happily in the new land." To help Maggie and Hal understand, Lady K quickly drew a map and acquainted them with the New Land beyond the Great Divide, while summarizing the four key cultural changes:

- loss of enclosed personal space

- reduced size of individual spaces

- loss of permanent habitats for some residents

- far more open and transparent landscape

The Dowager and Lord Badger nodded in agreement as they heard the news repeated, and asked in amazing unison, "But how can we get them to accept this change when we don't even understand it ourselves?"

"What we need," she said to the other provincial leaders, "what we need more than anything is a Change Management Plan."

"A what kind of plan? Sounds expensive to me!" exclaimed Hal, as Dowager O grunted in agreement.

Lady K was not discouraged. She pulled a faded and worn notebook out of her pouch and said excitedly, "I had almost forgotten this class I took at Crimson University called *Running with Scissors: Leading Change is Risky Business*. But last night, I could hear Professor Owl's wise hoot: 'As provincial leaders, we prepare new lands for the creatures. As change managers, we prepare creatures for the new land.'[2] You see, we can't relocate our citizens to the New Land and expect them to instinctively understand how to adjust their old habits and behaviors to live there peacefully! As leaders, it is our responsible to *prepare them* for the New Land!"

"So what you're saying is that we each need TWO plans by next week? One for the move itself, and another for the, what did you call it...?" the Dowager weakly inquired, already feeling overwhelmed.

"A Change Management plan," answered Lady K patiently. "But I actually think we need one holistic Change Management plan, for our three provinces to follow. I'd be willing to draft the strategy for review before we present to the King. Here, look at what I found. We can use this as the basic framework."

The four leaned in as Lady K opened her tattered textbook to a page called "The Eight Steps to Creating Change," written by Penquin John P. Kotter.[3] The eight steps were very clearly stated:

1) Establish a Sense of Urgency

2) Create a Guiding Coalition

3) Develop Vision and Strategy

4) Communicate Change Vision

5) Empower Broad-Based Action

6) Generate Short-Term Wins

7) Consolidate and Build on Gains

8) Anchor New Approaches (Make it Stick!)

Abruptly, Lord Badger jumped up, almost knocking Maggie off her perch. He loved lists! Forgetting his apprehensions, he exclaimed, "This is good stuff! In fact, we already have a head start on this list. What could be more urgent than moving in six months?! We can check off #1!"

The Dowager, catching his excitement, added, "I think the five of us are the Guiding Coalition mentioned in #2. And Lady K, you already said you'll draft #3, the Vision and Strategy, to share with the King."

The Eight Steps to Creating Change
by John P. Kotter [3]

1. Establish a Sense of Urgency
2. Create a Guiding Coalition
3. Develop Vision and Strategy
4. Communicate Change Vision
✳ 5. Empower Broad-Based Action ✳
6. Generate Short-Term Wins
7. Consolidate and Build on Gains
8. Anchor New Approaches (Make it Stick!)

[3] John P. Kotter (1996).
Leading Change.
Harvard Business School Press

Maggie excitedly exclaimed, "And I can lead #4 since I'm all about Communication."

At this point, Lady K pointed to her notes and showed the red asterisks around #5, Empower Broad-Based Action. "It's imperative that, for this plan to work, the mighty and the small of the Kingdom must become invested in the process and work together for the change. They can identify the real challenges and day-to-day realities that our field workers experience. They must feel, and actually be, empowered."

Hal the Honeybee was buzzing about with excitement. "That's what I'm talking about! That's the way to increase productivity! When creatures understand the reasons behind the change, they can work collaboratively to problem solve and become part of the solution, rather than the problem. And they can perhaps pilot their new ideas which would accomplish #6, to Generate Short Term Wins."

At this point, Maggie chirped in. "Then I can help with #7 and build momentum based upon early successes, and that always creates good will and especially good press!"

Now Lord Badger, feeling the need to assert his leadership once again, volunteered, "And I'm determined to help with #8, as we anchor our new behaviors and 'make them stick' when we get to the New Land." Lady K gently added, "Yes, and I think all of us will want to participate in #8."

They collectively grew silent, and took one long deep breath. As Lady K looked at the others, she realized that all were smiling for the first time since hearing the news.

Then Lord Badger's face changed. "But what will the King say? What if he won't go for it? I can't believe I'm even saying this, but what if he roars 'My subjects will move and will adapt simply because I say so!'"

Abruptly, they were interrupted by a bellowing roar behind them. "That certainly does sound like something I've been known to say!" They jumped up to face their King.

"How long have you've been listening?" Lady K asked, sounding far more confident than she felt.

The King chuckled and said, "Long enough to know that I certainly put the right ones in charge of our Bold Cultural Change. And Lord Badger, you were right to wonder if I would embrace a Change Management plan."

The King's voice grew quiet as he uttered his next words. "Frankly, I've been very worried about the success of our relocation, based upon my grandmother's story about leaving her birthplace. I purposely didn't mention this yesterday, but half of that Kingdom never made it across the Great Divide. The half that remained did so because they rebelled against being told to do something. Some left for a different Kingdom. Some formed their own small fiefdoms. And some simply withered away and perished in the fires, not willing to face the inevitable changes."

The King continued, "But as I listen to this thing called Change Management, I realize that is the key success factor missing from my grandmother's story. It's time to learn from past mistakes. We must include Change Management in our strategy plans! As my ancestors could attest, it would be far riskier to NOT include Change Management." The King added, "You have provided wise counsel today, my friends. Let's begin at once!"

The members of the newly formed Guiding Coalition knew there was much work ahead, but with Change Management as part of their overall strategy, they were confident they would be able to engage acceptance of the Kingdom's Bold Cultural Change across the Great Divide.

Part Two

The Hard Work of Change

Early the next morning Lady K gathered her class notes, tattered textbook, and rough draft of the K Province relocation plan. Her job was to draft an outline of the Change Management Vision and Strategy to review with the other members of the Guiding Coalition that evening. She poured a tall cup of coffee and took a seat on her back porch overlooking the lake and nearby meadows. She sat quietly and thought about all of the changes that were to come. There would be disruption to personal comfort as well as professional behavior. There would be new alliances forged and old ones abandoned. She opened her class notes and found Professor Owl's wise words:

"Change is hard because we overestimate what we have, and we underestimate what we are about to get."[4]

Lady K studied more of her notes. She remembered the **bell curve prediction of change**, with a few early adopters and a few resisters at the ends, while most would fall in the middle. Her eyes focused on the large ball near the resister end. The large ball represented the Power of Change Management, pushing the arc of the bell curve into the acceptance side.

She recalled that Change Management programs need to be aligned with the overarching project schedule, highlighting important milestones and opportunities. Randomly opening her textbook to a page, she drew a quick sharp breath when she read the advice about the importance of pilot projects. Hmmm. **"Pilot projects are best accomplished when Change Management begins very early in the process, so that ideas can be tested and refinements can be made before final design and implementation."** She remembered Hal the Honeybee was all abuzz about piloting new ideas. But would they have time for a pilot project? She flagged this idea for discussion with her colleagues that evening.

Turning to the next chapter in her textbook, Lady K reviewed the critical steps to making a case for implementing a Change Management program. As she reviewed the four components of a business case, Lady K thought it would be wise to include them in her Vision and Strategy draft:

- Consider the link to organizational goals and mission

- Conduct research to support Change Management, including Animal Resource metrics, best practices, and executive-suite hot buttons

- Determine scope and scale of the Change Management program

- Calculate return on investment

Even though the King accepted the need for a Change Management program, there would be plenty who might question why they were taking this path. "Yes," she nodded to herself, "we need to clearly articulate the case for our Change Management program." She expected that Hal would be especially delighted to provide some Animal Resource metrics and best practices.

The thought of Hal made her consider the approach she would take that evening. It would be important to involve the other four members of the Guiding Coalition in developing the Vision and Strategy. Just as they will be involving members of the kingdom in the Change Management process itself by forming a Change Agent Committee, Lady K understood that she needed to involve her colleagues in visioning the Change Management program. The more creatures have a voice in the process, the more they own it. She needed to be careful to draft enough of an outline to keep them on track this evening, but she needed to resist the urge to "do it" for them.

Lady K outlined an agenda for the Visioning and Strategy meeting with the Guiding Coalition:

1) Provide Change Management overview to align understanding and expectations

2) Review opportunities for change and key challenges, specific to each Province, including space relationships and processes that shape behavior

3) Review purpose of Change Agent Committee and highlight specific responsibilities; brainstorm list of possible members from each province

4) Outline "six-months until we move" schedule, understand upcoming milestones, consider pilot project, anticipate Change Agent Committee involvement, and outline immediate next steps

5) Determine broad goals and success factors for Change Management

Satisfied that she was ready, she packed up her notes, tattered textbook, a few flipchart pages, and some markers, and placed them in her pouch.

It took Lady K almost an hour to hop to the Dowager's home in the O Province. Although she could cover great distances in a short time, she had to stop several times along the way, flagged down and questioned by worried residents of the K Province. Even residents of the O Province recognized her and wanted her to stop mid-hop to hear their concerns. But she had to press on, fully aware that she would now be late for the meeting.

At last Lady K arrived at the Dowager's front door. Before she could knock, the door was opened by the butler, who motioned her into the spacious drawing room. Lady K paused as she entered and surveyed the room's occupants. Maggie Magpie was nervously munching on sunflower seeds, while the Dowager was pacing anxiously near the window. Hal the Honeybee buzzed about muttering rants about lost utilization rates and increasing operational costs.

"My apologies for being late. I was … "

"Good grief! Oh my word! I mean …" Lady K was interrupted by a wide-eyed and harried Lord Badger who barged into the room, almost toppling a large vase of flowers. Watching the others, he realized he had just rudely interrupted Lady K. "I'm so sorry Lady K." Still catching his breath, he added, "I'm just frustrated that I've arrived so late. I left in plenty of time but did not anticipate the barrage of inquiries awaiting me at every turn. My province residents are demanding answers that I can't give. Do continue." And with that, Lord Badger collapsed onto an ottoman.

The Dowager nodded to Lady K, who continued, "I was simply explaining that I arrived late for the same reasons. We all have lots of residents who are in need of information, and soon!" The kangaroo paused, and addressed the honeybee, who was still buzzing about. "Hal, you are absolutely correct about productivity loss, and it's not only our residents, but us too!" Abruptly, Hal landed on a flower petal, looking relieved that his message had been heard.

The Dowager welcomed the latecomers and invited all to take a seat in the dining room. Lady K noted with pleasure that the ostrich had thoughtfully prepared for this important strategy meeting of the Guiding Coalition by providing ample refreshments, flipcharts, markers, sticky notes, and other materials essential to brainstorming.

The five leaders took their seats. All eyes turned to Lady K, who had positioned herself at the head of the table. She smiled and began by outlining the purpose and goals of this meeting. "We are gathered tonight as members of the Guiding Coalition to brainstorm the Vision and Strategy for our Change Management Program, which will fulfill step number three of the eight steps to creating change. I've prepared an agenda to keep us on track."

Addressing the first agenda item, Lady K summarized the need for Change Management. "Change Management will lead our residents from **where they are to where they need to be.** There are many benefits of implementing a Change Management Program." As she described the benefits, Maggie listed them on the flipchart:

- **Centralizes communications** for the relocation

- Maintains **high productivity**, allowing leaders as well as residents to **stay focused** on real priorities

- **Alerts** senior leadership to important issues for early resolution

- **Negates rumor mill** and gossip

- Promotes **good will**

- Offers residents a more **holistic** view

- **Eases emotional transition** to a new and different culture

Next, the group focused on opportunities for change as well as key challenges facing their residents. Each province leader listed their concerns regarding space relationships and the behavior changes that they anticipated on their flipcharts. While many areas overlapped, there were also unique provincial challenges. Lord Badger was especially concerned about the northwestern residents of the B Province, who presently enjoyed an abundance of space.

After listing key concerns and challenges, Lady K made sure they focused on the positive side of change by brainstorming benefits that would result from the relocation. Maggie Magpie was especially helpful by suggesting how life might improve in their new land. Hal the Honeybee already anticipated improved productivity and operational savings, and presented a few spreadsheets of compelling metrics, despite his incessant worries about the potential for labor strikes if the creatures did not buy into the change. The others were genuinely pleased that he had explored these possibilities, and realized that his work could provide important incentives for the residents as well as the King.

An hour had already slipped by when Lady K stood to reiterate the importance of the next item, the Change Agent Committee. "Friends, I'm especially excited to describe the purpose of the Change Agent Committee and highlight members' responsibilities. While we won't have time this evening to develop a comprehensive list of possible committee members from each province, I'm hopeful that we can at least brainstorm a few names, especially some early adopters and some resisters."

"Did you say resisters? Are you crazy?!!! I've got enough challenges in the B Province without inviting resisters to stir up trouble!" exclaimed Lord Badger. The Dowager nodded her agreement while Maggie chirped nervously. Hal began to buzz about, his brows furrowed with worry.

Lady K winced, "Okay. Let's break for a few minutes and then I'll explain the big picture view of the Change Agent Committee."

Lady K turned her back and began drawing on a flipchart. The others, some still muttering, went to refill their teacups. When they returned, they saw that Lady K had drawn a bell curve, with a large ball pushing against one end of the curve.

"Generally speaking, if we graph the acceptance of change, we find that it resembles a bell curve: a few resisters and a few early adopters at either end, and the majority of creatures in-between. An effective Change Management program, represented by this large ball, can shift that curve so that more fall into the acceptance side, rather than the resistance side." Her colleagues nodded their understanding.

Lady K continued, drawing a couple of up and down arrows as she spoke. "For a Change Management program to succeed, it must be implemented Top-Down *and* Bottom-Up. If it's just Top Down, with the King commanding it, the entire kingdom is not likely to buy in, which is what happened when the King's grandmother migrated many years ago. If it's just Bottom-Up, then creatures seek change without leadership, which results in chaos, revolution, and failed initiatives. When we engage both Top-Down and Bottom-Up, it's a win-win." Heads nodded again in agreement.

"To truly engage everyone in our change program, we need to invite naysayers into our process." She pointed to the end of the bell curve, near the large ball. "If we don't, it excludes a representative segment of our population. But more than that,

how powerful would it be if we engage naysayers and they actually become *proponents* of change, rather than *opponents*? If we exclude the resisters, they'll always remain opposed. But if we include them, we stand a very good chance of changing their minds because we have given them a voice, we have listened to their voice, we have adjusted some of our proposals due to their input, and they have adjusted their thinking because they were heard. It's another win-win." She paused, hoping her words were sinking in.

Rising, Dowager O was the first to speak, "Thank you Lady K. I now understand why resisters will be important to include. To be honest, I myself have never adapted well to change. With time, I do come around, although the process can be quite painful. When I think of the times that I have adjusted more readily, it was because I had a voice in the process."

Even Lord Badger sniffed agreement as the Dowager took her seat. Then he asked, "So tell us more about the role and purpose of the Change Agent Committee, so that we may begin to think of possible members."

Lady K eagerly reached for her class notes and textbook and read aloud while Maggie took notes on the flipchart. "Ideally, twelve to eighteen primary members should be appointed to serve on the Change Agent Committee. They will serve as liaisons during regularly scheduled meetings of the Change Agent Committee, representing all tribes involved in the relocation. They will be responsible for communicating the concerns and questions of their tribes, and likewise, communicating back to their tribes regarding the programs and activities surrounding the Bold Cultural Change. The Change Agent Committee should be comprised of a diverse mix of ages, species, and experience. However, it is best to avoid selecting residents from high leadership positions because the lowliest in the kingdom are often hesitant to speak up in their presence. A few resisters and early adopters should also be included, with the majority being in the middle when it comes to accepting change. Furthermore, each committee member should have a designated alternate in case the member can't attend because of illness or vacation. Sometimes both primaries and alternates should attend a meeting of particular significance."

Lord Badger asked, "Since my province is the largest, will we have more representation?"

Hal the Honeybee buzzed, "How often will the Change Agent Committee members meet, and how will this impact overall productivity?"

Maggie chirped, "Who will lead these meetings? Will it be one of us and will I still be in charge of communications?"

The Dowager asked, "Why is the group limited to no more than eighteen members? We have at least one hundred different species in the O Province, so how will they all receive adequate representation?"

Lady K acknowledged that these were all good questions, and that they would need to work together to determine the answers. They decided to schedule another meeting for the next day to resolve these questions, since they still had more to cover that evening to complete the Vision and Strategy. But they all committed to bring names for the Change Agent Committee to the next day's meeting.

After a brief break to watch a beautiful sunset from the Dowager's terrace, Lady K introduced the fourth agenda item. "It is time to outline our six-month move schedule. We need to anticipate major milestones, and I hope we can include a pilot project to test some of the new cultural changes and behaviors."

Hal spoke up immediately, rolling out a long parchment for all to see. "I took the liberty to draft a rough move schedule, considering each of the provinces and how we might phase the moves. I took into account the weather patterns over the next six months, the busy periods of a few of our tribes, and the times when it is treacherous to cross the Great Divide. But I didn't know where to insert the pilot project, because we haven't discussed what that might be."

Lord Badger looked up. "I'm quite impressed, Hal. You even acknowledge in your schedule the extra time it will take for our smallest in the northwest B Province to make the trek across our challenging hills and valleys."

The Dowager nodded, adding, "And you remembered the dry spell that comes with the summer solstice. That's an important milestone."

Maggie agreed, "And although you don't give details, you have noted that a communications plan must be launched almost immediately. That's excellent!"

Lady K said, "Does anyone object to this draft schedule being included in our Vision and Strategy? We will still have time to study and finesse, but if no one objects, I suggest we give thought to a pilot project and whether we have time to include one in this schedule."

Hal urgently replied, "We absolutely must find a way to include a pilot project in our schedule! It's the best way get our residents to test new ideas, understand the challenges, and work collaboratively to solve problems and become part of the solution. If I understand correctly, pilot projects are an effective way to generate short term wins, which is number six in our eight steps to change, right?" The others nodded in agreement, somewhat amused by Hal's impassioned support of the pilot idea.

The next half hour flew by quickly as the group explored pilot possibilities. First, they easily agreed that the ideal pilot would simulate all four characteristics of the Bold Cultural Change: loss of enclosed personal space, reduced size of individual spaces, loss of permanent habitats for some residents, and an open terrain. The hard part was selecting an area in the Kingdom that could be used as a pilot space, then identifying members of the Kingdom who would be willing to participate.

Abruptly, Hal left the group and buzzed into the drawing room. He called the others in to examine a map of the Kingdom above the Dowager's fireplace and buzzed with excitement as he pointed to an area called Central Park, straddling the O and B Provinces.

"Look here!" exclaimed the honeybee, "Central Park has several landscape features similar to the New Land. It's exceptionally transparent on its northeast corner due to open fields for sports activities. With a small amount of work, this half of the park in the B Province could be transformed to accommodate our pilot participants. We could leave the other half of the park open for leisure activities. Plus this park is centrally located in our Kingdom and would allow both the mighty and small to visit to observe and give their opinions. What do you think?"

"Well, I don't like it at all," the badger bristled. "You just eliminated the entire piece of the park that resides in the B Province. Everyone knows that section of the park plays host to no less than one hundred games each weekend, from football to baseball to bocci. Games are played by many members of the Kingdom, my own son included, fostering healthy competition and camaraderie among our provinces. Surely we can find a better location!"

Lord Badger pushed them out of the way, and began scanning the map for suitable alternatives After several minutes punctuated by audible grunts and heavy sighs, he turned to his fellow leaders and grudgingly admitted that he could not identify a better location. The room was quiet. Lady K gently placed her paw on the badger's shoulder and suggested that they all return to the dining room. As they gathered once again around Hal's schedule, she acknowledged, "Sometimes change is very hard indeed to accept. All of us as leaders, and all of the Kingdom's creatures, will be experiencing significant change, even before we move. Lord Badger has expressed what many of us are feeling." Lady K gave him an assuring nod. He managed a weak smile.

She continued, "I consider this a healthy dialogue, and it's just one of many in the coming months. But our thoughtful collaboration will lead to creative solutions, and remember, the Change Agent Committee will be helping us. As you consider names to submit tomorrow, use the challenging moments of these last few minutes to inspire you to select residents that are good problem solvers as well as good communicators."

Satisfied that they had decided on a suitable pilot location, albeit with challenges yet to be resolved, the five focused on who the pilot participants might be. Lord Badger suggested that a reasonable percentage of the total population of each species in each province should participate. Hal consulted his Animal

Resource spreadsheets and offered approximate numbers per species per province. The three provincial leaders committed to drafting a list of participants for review at tomorrow's meeting. They agreed that at least one pilot member from each province should serve on the Change Agent Committee, so that the pilot group also had representation.

Hal hovered over his draft project schedule, making notes to reflect their decisions. "Hey, does this seem right to you? I'm adding the Pilot Project to occur very early in the process so that we can learn from our experience and implement necessary changes when we design our New Land. Yikes, this will be very fast tracked!" He pointed to the first two months of the schedule.

Hal continued, "I've added that the King needs to appoint an overall Project Manager as well as a Project Designer. Both will need to focus on the fast-track pilot project as well as the New Land project. These appointments will need to occur next week in order to stay on track."

"But what about someone to lead the Change Management program?" Maggie asked.

All eyes turned to Lady K. "That's a very good question," the kangaroo replied. "Like the Dowager and Lord Badger, I'm already busy with provincial leadership and our Guiding Coalition. So as much as I'm tempted to lead the Change

Management program, I don't believe I have the time to do it justice."

"Then who will lead it?" asked the Dowager.

Lady K replied, "One of my colleagues from graduate school lives in the B Province, in the northwestern territory. We collaborated on several projects while at Crimson University. She is a team player, decisive when appropriate, and keeps a positive attitude even in the face of adversity."

Lord Badger grinned at her, "You must mean Joy the Giraffe! Joy would be an excellent choice! How about you and I pay her a visit tomorrow just prior to our Guiding Coalition meeting? In fact, perhaps we can suggest that she attend it with us." The others nodded in agreement. Even the Dowager seemed relieved.

Lady K noted that they had one last agenda item left, but she could read the faces of her colleagues and knew that their energy was draining quickly. "I see that the hour is very late," she announced. "May I propose that we begin tomorrow's meeting with our remaining agenda item, to outline the broad goals and success factors for Change Management? That way, if she accepts our offer, we could include Joy in the discussion. She could at least listen, and maybe she'll have a few ideas to offer, as well as suggestions for the Change Agent Committee."

Hal buzzed his relief and agreement, while Maggie stifled a

yawn. Lord Badger was already at the door saying his goodbyes before the Dowager could ring for her butler. They all agreed to meet the next afternoon at Lord Badger's brownstone across from Central Park, and were hopeful that Lady K and the badger would be bringing Joy to meet them.

~~~~~~~~~~

The sun was shining the next day when Hal and Maggie arrived at Lord Badger's home. They had chosen to fly together, arriving early enough to watch one of the football games from a limb in Central Park. Of course, they couldn't help but brainstorm ideas about the Pilot Project from their high vantage point as they made mental notes of desirable characteristics as well as challenging features.

Lord Badger's butler answered the door and escorted them to the back courtyard, where they were surprised to find the Dowager already there and sipping tea alone. "Lord Badger and Lady K are slightly delayed, according to The Philippe Meister," explained the butler. No more needed to be said, since everyone knew that the word of the Kingdom's swiftest and most reliable carrier pigeon could be trusted.

Maggie felt compelled to ask, "Did The Meister mention if they are being accompanied by anyone else?"

"He did not say," the butler replied, closing the French doors.

Before they could wonder aloud, they heard soft voices in the corner of the courtyard. Turning, they could not help but notice the tall graceful movements of a long lean giraffe, flanked on either side by Lady K and Lord Badger. While their host secured the back gate, Lady K introduced Joy to the others. Warm smiles and greetings were exchanged, and Lord Badger explained that the back alley enabled them to arrive without much attention. "It's been a rather long journey today, and we were stopped several times by many inquisitive residents."

"Yes indeed!" said Joy. "And it gave me the chance to learn about this Change Management program. I'm delighted that you've invited me to lead this effort. We need to begin immediately!"

"Time to get to work then!" said the host, and motioned for them to gather around the long table. Like the Dowager, he had made appropriate preparations for a brainstorming session. Lady K listed goals of the meeting on the flipchart while Hal rolled out his parchment schedule. Joy's long neck stretched over the entire length of the schedule, and she nodded with understanding.

Lady K invited Joy to share the head of the table. The two change experts worked seamlessly, facilitating the group's discussion as though it had only been ten hours rather than ten years since they collaborated at university.

Before long the six leaders had drafted the broad goals and success factors for their Change Management program, which was the final task to completing the Vision and Strategy. Energy was high, and Joy's objective opinions were extremely helpful.

Joy asked if she could summarize the goals and success factors for the group, partially to test her own understanding. "We began an hour ago by asking ourselves: How will we define success in six months, following our move to the New Land? We pictured ourselves in this New Land, and what changes will occur. And we described, in great detail, what success will look like." Heads nodded.

She continued, "With the cultural changes in mind, we drafted broad goals around five themes:

1) Leverage Physical Space for the Greater Good

2) Increase Operational Efficiencies

3) Encourage Hoarding Reductions

4) Provide Timely Communications

5) Ensure Unified and Happy Residents

"Each of these goals has a specific Change Management objective associated with it," Joy said, pointing to each of the five flipchart pages taped to the courtyard walls. Hal especially

buzzed about flipchart number two, while Maggie chirped her pleasure about flipchart number four.

Joy paused, waiting for comments. Lady K was the first to speak. "Look at what we've accomplished! This is exactly what I had hoped we would complete this afternoon. We still have details to discuss regarding the Change Agent Committee and the Pilot Project in Central Park. I don't want to rush us, but does this feel right to everyone else?"

The Dowager rose, stretched her long legs, and stated, "This really makes it clear where we should focus our efforts, and how we will define success. I especially like that we worded the goals in future tense, and in a positive tone. The King will like that as well!"

"I concur," said Lord Badger. "Now it's time to address the next topics!"

First, the group focused on the names each had brought for the Change Agent Committee. It took a bit of work to narrow the list down to eighteen primary members, and eighteen alternates. Because they wanted the Pilot Project to have representation, they decided to brainstorm those names at the same time. They had to balance ages, species, tribe affiliation, and resisters vs. early adopters. By the time they were done, the flipcharts were a mess of names, markings, asterisks, and scratch-outs.

Satisfied that they had a solid group of change agents, they decided to brainstorm the specific goals and opportunities for the Pilot Project. Hal, master of efficiency, had thought to bring along plans of Central Park. He and Maggie shared notes from their earlier limb watching. Even Lord Badger seemed to be genuinely engaged in the possibilities in spite of the loss of ball fields and B Province parklands. They decided on approximate population densities and narrowed their list of Pilot participant names. Broad goals were outlined using the four key areas of cultural change. Hal reminded them that the King would be appointing a Project Designer, who would take their goals and preliminary ideas into consideration.

Lord Badger felt a tug on his knee. "Dad," whispered a small badger, "You haven't forgotten about our team practice have you?"

"Oh my goodness! Is it that time already?" exclaimed the older badger. He jumped up, forgetting his manners, and then paused as Joy the Giraffe leaned down and nuzzled his son's head.

"Well, hello there, Buzz. It's been awhile since I've seen you. Still playing wide receiver?"

"Yes ma'am," replied Buzz excitedly. "If you'd like, you can come see our games every weekend, right across the street in Central Park. My dad is our coach. We play the Ravens tribe from the O Province this Saturday. Right Dad?"

"Uhhh....that's right, son," said Lord Badger, relieved to see that Hal was folding the map of Central Park while Lady K had already taken down the pages of flipcharts.

Lady K announced, "Friends, we are finished for today. Great work! It's time to get going and let Lord Badger and Buzz enjoy their football."

~~~~~~~~~~

The next morning, Lady K rose early to put the finishing touches on her presentation. As she hopped to the King's lair, she reviewed in her mind the key points of the Change Management Vision and Strategy. She decided she should begin by reminding the King of the eight steps, and briefly summarize what the Guiding Coalition had done in the last two days. Here it was already Day Five, and the King was expecting comprehensive relocation plans the day after tomorrow. She wasn't worried— their focus on Change Management planning was helping to shape their plans for the relocation.

The King was waiting for her on his high terrace. He invited her to sit and was intrigued as she pulled the flipchart pages and a map out of her pouch.

"King Lion, your Guiding Coalition for Change Management has met for many hours since the Savanna Hall announcement to develop the Vision and Strategy for our Change Management program, with keen awareness of the four key cultural changes that await our residents." Lady K began. "As you will remember, Vision and Strategy is step number three of the eight essential steps to change." She pointed to the listing of the eight steps. The King nodded.

Lady K continued with growing confidence. "Not only have we drafted the Vision and Strategy for your review, but I'm prepared to share with you our preliminary thoughts on how we plan to communicate the vision, empower the residents through a Change Agent Committee, and pilot a project to generate short-term wins, which will take us through step number six."

The King raised his eyebrows as the kangaroo proceeded to unfold several flipchart pages. One by one, she reviewed the key components of the Vision and Strategy: Change Management overview; provincial opportunities and challenges; Change Agent Committee purpose and membership; project schedule; and goals and success factors for Change Management.

The King studied the flipchart pages. "I am pleased to see that you have worded the goals in future tense, and in a positive tone." Lady K smiled, remembering the Dowager mentioning the King's preferences. The King asked for more information about the "no hoarding" policy and the Kingdom Etiquette Guidelines. Satisfied that the Guiding Coalition had thoughtfully developed the five goals, the King turned his attention to the Change Agent Committee and the pilot project.

Lady K explained the composition of the Change Agent Committee, as well as its purpose and responsibilities. The King nodded, impressed with her thoroughness and logic. She then presented the list of eighteen primary members and eighteen alternates. He especially appreciated the rationale behind inviting a few resisters to the table.

"So far, so good," stated the King. "Please continue, and tell me about this pilot project. Who will be participating, and where in the Kingdom do you plan to model the New Land?"

Lady K carefully unfolded Hal's map of Central Park. The King's eyes narrowed as he recognized the prized ball fields and track on the northeast side, and the markings that designated this region for the pilot project. Lady K, not noticing his reaction, spoke for several minutes before realizing that the King was uncharacteristically quiet. She paused.

"Do you mean to tell me that we will have to give up the one place that brings us together as a Kingdom, the mighty and the small, the players and the spectators? This is sacred land!" The King bellowed. "Furthermore, I cannot believe that Lord Badger approved this idea."

Unflustered, Lady K explained Lord Badger's initial reaction, his determination to find an alternate location, and his eventual acceptance that this was indeed the only suitable location. The King also insisted on poring over the map looking for another site and, like his advisor, could find none.

Finally the King spoke. "I guess I too am having a hard time with change. But the Guiding Coalition is right. This is the best place for our pilot project. In fact, I cannot find fault with any of your Vision and Strategy. Please continue, Lady K."

Breathing a sigh of relief, Lady K reviewed Hal's schedule, including the notations about the King needing to appoint a Project Manager and a Project Designer. She pointed out that the pilot project was fast-tracked to test ideas for application in the New Land. Lady K also told the King about Joy the Giraffe, the Guiding Coalition's choice to lead the Change Management effort.

"What we need now are your recommendations for the Project Manager and Project Designer," Lady K stated. "We need to get them on board immediately, especially since each Province Leader owes you a relocation plan in just two days and could surely benefit from wise counsel from professionals."

The King considered past experiences with various professionals in his Kingdom. After a few minutes he turned to Lady K and announced his choices.

"To fill the position of Project Manager, I appoint Whitney the Wildebeest from the O Province," the King began. "Whitney has that rare combination of technical know-how and highly developed communication skills. He's an outstanding task manager, and a whiz with schedules and spreadsheets that will impress even Hal the Honeybee. He's a good listener and can motivate even the slowest snail in the Kingdom. Maggie has worked with Whitney on previous projects and has always praised his ability to communicate at all levels, mighty and small."

Lady K was convinced. "Fabulous! Do you have ideas for the Project Designer?

"Yes, but I think that we need two designers," the King replied. "According to the schedule, we really have two fast-tracked projects: The Pilot and the New Land. I believe we could benefit from two designers so they can focus and respond quickly." Lady K nodded, appreciating his wisdom.

The King continued, "I will appoint John Jay the Butterfly to design our pilot in Central Park, where he has resided for all of his life, from caterpillar to the beautiful Citrus Swallowtail that we recognize today." Lady K bobbed in agreement, having known John Jay from his early days in the cocoon.

The King continued, "And for our New Land, I will appoint Perry the Zebra as our designer. Not only does Perry understand the importance of aesthetics and outward beauty, she also designs for optimal functionality, a quality we will surely need as we move to a land where space is at a premium. Furthermore, Perry grew up hearing the same stories that I did about the land across the Great Divide. She understands what we are gaining and what features we will be losing when we relocate." Lady K smiled, acknowledging the thoughtfulness of the King's selection.

Pleased with his decisions, the King sent for The Philippe Meister, the carrier pigeon, to summon the three new appointees to the Kingdom for high tea that afternoon. He asked Lady K to invite the other members of the Guiding Coalition to join them, along with Joy the Giraffe. Time was of the essence, and they needed a work session with experts to develop their relocation plans.

~~~~~~~~~~

The sun was still high in the sky when the five members of the Guiding Coalition arrived at the King's gate. Joy made the journey with them, and they met up with Whitney the Wildebeest at the edge of the path. The seven turned as they heard laughter behind them. John Jay the Butterfly was hitching a ride on the back of Perry the Zebra, and the two designers were engaged in light-hearted humor and banter. The others couldn't help but smile at their antics. Together, they were welcomed onto the King's terrace.

The King warmly greeted his nine loyal subjects, thinking to himself that he was indeed surrounded by the best and the brightest. He needed these leaders to protect and advance the Kingdom. After a few words of introduction, and acknowledgement of the importance of the task at hand, the

King announced, "I look forward to reviewing your preliminary relocation plans over dinner and wine." With a swish of his tail, the King left.

Wasting no time, the Guiding Coalition briefed the three new appointees on the four key cultural changes, the need for Change Management, the eight steps of change, the Vision and Strategy (including the five goals), the Change Agent Committee, and the Pilot Project. Like Joy the Giraffe, they were all quick learners.

Whitney demonstrated his project management skills, volunteering to work with Hal on fine tuning the drafted project schedules to include specific provincial milestones as well as key due dates for the pilot project. John Jay didn't waste any time putting his knowledge of Central Park to work, allaying any remaining fears that Lord Badger may have had regarding a workable design. Likewise, Perry began sketching ideas on tracing parchment overlaid on top of the King's ancient map of the region east of the Great Divide. The three provincial leaders huddled to outline their individual, yet related, relocation plans, while Maggie flew from map to plan to schedule to map to plan and roundabout again, making notes for a rough communications plan. Joy listened to all conversations, scribbling ideas on a large parchment about possible Change Management activities by the Change Agent Committee to parallel the design and construction projects.

The nine were ready for the King by the time the dinner gong had sounded. They were escorted into his spacious dining cave, where shadows from the chandelier and torchieres danced on the ceiling. The mood was light and cheery, and the King couldn't help but smile as they entered.

"I can see already that you have experienced success. As the dinner courses begin, please share your relocations plans," the King said, passing a bottle of wine to Lady K at his right.

Hal and Whitney were the first to present since it was important that the overall project schedule be understood. The schedule illustrated their "sense of urgency," with the countdown of six months for the ultimate move, but also a shorter countdown for the fast-tracked pilot project. Next, John Jay presented his detailed design of the B Province portion of Central Park, accommodating all of the intended population while incorporating simulated New Land features. He was delighted to see that the King and Lord Badger were nodding their approval, since he had been tipped off by Lady K that they were the two he needed to win over.

Then Perry stood, asking Hal and John Jay to hold her colorful parchment sketches of the eastern region of the Great Divide. She described the districts, nodes, pathways, edges, and landmarks that could be created, optimizing the features of the New Land while supporting the new population densities. She incorporated prospect and refuge, necessary survival strategies for the Kingdom's mighty and small, and highlighted the natural elements that would appeal to the residents, many of which didn't exist where they lived now. Joy listened attentively, noting topics for the Change Agent Committee meetings. Maggie perched nearby, whispering additional ideas into her ear regarding communication.

When Perry was finished, the room was silent. No one was eating. Eyes were wide. Expressions were mixed. Perry held her breath. Then all at once, the entire table literally jumped as everyone rose to their feet, paws, and wings.

"I can't believe I'm saying this, but I want to move there!"

"Exactly my thinking! Wow!"

"In just a few hours, you've managed to address all of my unstated worries! How did you know?"

The King shook his mane with pleasure, and even the Badger sported a toothy grin.

Joy stated the obvious. "Your design has given us so much to work with. I'm fully aware that we still have hurdles to overcome, but you have illustrated several ways that our lives will actually improve when we move to the New Land. I can already anticipate that we'll want you to present at one of the early meetings of the Change Agent Committee!"

Perry humbly thanked them, took her seat, and finally exhaled. She sneaked a wink to John Jay, who gave her the wing up.

Next, the three Provincial leaders outlined their relocation plans, which now seemed not as daunting with the hopeful outlook provided by their designer. Whitney elaborated on some of the project management strategies that would accompany portions of their plans, mostly related to weather conditions and logistical considerations. The King followed along, nodding his approval.

Finally, Maggie flew to the chandelier and chirped her ideas for the overall communications plan. She would be handling the communications for the Change Management and provincial relocation plans, so she would need to coordinate seamlessly with her eight colleagues. It would be complex at times, but she had her methods and was trustworthy.

The King pushed back his chair and stood as he roared, "Well done! And may I point out that you completed your relocation plans ahead of deadline!"

Lady K, the Dowager, and Lord Badger looked at each other in amazement. Yes they had! Two whole days early!

Maggie said excitedly, "We need to coordinate the timing of the messaging. We need to share your plans with your provinces. How about..." She was interrupted by the King.

"Maggie, I love your dedication and your enthusiasm," stated the

King, with affection. "But I think this can wait until morning. It's late, and you have all completed amazing work tonight. Let them sleep on it. What do you say?"

The magpie smiled sheepishly and agreed, then added, "But don't be surprised if I'm your wake-up chirp in the morning!"

The King laughed, and patted everyone on their backs as they left. Once outside the gate, the nine leaders cheered and engaged in a massive high five, being careful not to squish their flying members. The hard work would begin tomorrow, but for now, they were celebrating.

Part Three

Preparing Others for the Change

True to her word, Maggie visited each the three provincial leaders at the crack of dawn. By mid-morning she had drafted the messaging for the relocation plans for each leader to deliver in their respective provinces that afternoon. Maggie knew they had to also reassure residents that the King had things under control, and she wanted to deliver the news about the Change Management Program immediately following the relocation announcements. She decided to fly to Joy's home to consult with her before briefing the King. The flight to the western region gave the magpie the opportunity to survey the spacious and lush terrain that the residents would be leaving in a few short months, an important reminder of how great the change would be for many creatures.

Maggie found Joy sitting on her dock overlooking Lake Sniggle Snaggle. The giraffe was deep in thought, her long neck moving from side to side as she examined stacks of parchments. On the top of one stack, Maggie recognized the messiest flipchart page from their Change Agent Committee brainstorming session.

"Good morning Joy," tweeted the magpie brightly.

Startled, Joy looked up with surprised eyes, then laughed. "Take a perch, my feathered friend; your timing is perfect! I have been at this for hours, and need someone to bounce ideas off."

"And I need to consult with you about my communications plan, especially the immediate messaging," replied Maggie.

Before long, the two had outlined plans that were coordinated yet distinct. Maggie's communications plan would launch with the King endorsing the Change Management program in support of the three provincial relocation plans. His visible and vocal backing of the Change Management effort was necessary for several reasons. First, his support would reiterate that change is indeed coming, and is so big that the Kingdom needs a focused effort to assure success. Second, the King's endorsement would highlight the significance of the Change Agent Committee, comprised of residents appointed to serve as representatives of the mighty and small. Lastly, his endorsement would send a clear message that all residents would be involved in preparing for the change.

"In order for the Kingdom to really comprehend the importance of the Change Management program, I think the King needs to issue a royal proclamation," suggested Joy.

Maggie heartily agreed, "Great idea! That would certainly let our residents know this is serious business!" She made a note to pen the proclamation on official Kingdom rolled parchments. Her team of deputy magpies would make the announcements.

Joy's rough outline for the Change Management program included a Change Communications plan that Maggie would lead. The details of the Change Communications plan would be developed with input from the Change Agent Committee. A priority action on Joy's list was to have the King appoint the eighteen primary members and eighteen alternates.

"You know," Maggie said, "Let's give the change program a name and design a logo. That way, any communications related to our relocation will be obvious and all will know it's important."

Joy added enthusiastically, "Brainstorming the name could be one of the earliest responsibilities of the Change Agent Committee!"

"I can't think of a better way to engage them immediately and get them working towards a common goal," chirped Maggie. "Now I understand why you are preparing a rough outline rather than a detailed one. You really do intend for the change agents to participate in each step of the process."

Feeling satisfied that they each had a plan, they agreed to meet after Maggie briefed the King. The provincial leaders would deliver their independent relocation plans that afternoon to the residents of their respective provinces. Maggie would be seeking the King's commitment to issue the Change Management proclamation immediately following.

~~~~~~~~~~

"Hear ye, hear ye," tweeted the town criers throughout the Kingdom. "Be it known that the King endorses a comprehensive Change Management Program to begin immediately to prepare for the move across the Great Divide," the deputy magpies continued, making mention of the pending formation of a Change Agent Committee. Crowds gathered to hear the proclamations, and chattered excitedly about the news.

Kat the Leopard licked her lips in anticipation of juicy stories to include in the next issue of *The Sun*, the Kingdom's news journal. She snapped a few photos and then roamed the crowd to interview residents. She was grateful that Maggie Magpie had given her the early scoop. Kat had grown weary of the negative press that dominated the news the past week.

"What do you think about the King's appointment of Joy the Giraffe to lead this thing called Change Management?" Kat asked Pep the Porcupine, sitting on a branch in a nearby tree.

Startled, Pep's quills flared and then settled down as he replied, "I've never met Joy, so I can't say for sure. But I do like the idea of a Change Management program. I've been prickly all week about our upcoming move. I heard the Dowager deliver her relocation plan this afternoon, and I'm not convinced. I have lots of questions and concerns."

"Will the Change Agent Committee be your source for answers?" Kat pressed.

"That remains to be seen. I don't even know who our tribe's representative will be."

Just then, two carrier pigeons from The Philippe Meister's flock descended with authority onto the village square. The crowd grew quiet and made room for the esteemed messengers. One carrier pigeon delivered a small rolled parchment to Pep the Porcupine. The other approached JayEll the Gazelle, who was standing in the shade of a nearby tree. JayEll was highly respected in the O Province, known for his sharp analytical mind yet graceful delivery of opinion.

Pep and JayEll eyed one another and opened their parchments simultaneously, while Kat whipped out her camera, snapping away in hopes that she was catching late-breaking news. "So what does it say?" she asked excitedly, between clicks of her shutter.

The porcupine's surprised eyes were still staring at the parchment while the gazelle looked up and gracefully answered, "We've been summoned to the King's lair this evening to be sworn in as Change Agents. There will be thirty-six of us in total, representing all tribes across the three provinces. Our work begins tomorrow."

"Hooray," cheered the crowd. Kat looked up and noted a flock of carrier pigeons en route to other tribes across the Kingdom. She decided to head to the King's lair in hopes of being allowed to photograph the swearing-in ceremony.

~~~~~~~~~~

A whirlwind of activities occurred across the Kingdom following the swearing-in ceremony. Pleased with the positive press that Kat had provided in *The Sun* about the Change Agent Committee, Maggie asked the photojournalist to feature a regular column to keep residents informed about the move. Kat's editor was delighted, and reserved the front page for the column. Maggie instructed her deputy magpies to keep the photojournalist fully informed, hoping that the transparency would help them achieve goal number four, Timely Communications.

Kat was invited to attend the second meeting of the Change Agent Committee to observe and report on the group's activities. With introductions behind them, the change agents were anxious to provide feedback and suggestions, as well as have questions answered. Joy had an aggressive agenda, but knew it was wise to open the meeting by asking for questions.

Sarah the Shrew was the first to raise her paw. "My tribe is asking lots of questions about the New Land. They hear that it is much smaller, but they don't know how much smaller. Some are concerned there won't be enough water, while others are worried there won't be enough shade."

Harry the Hyena chimed in, "My grandfather left that land many years ago, and says it was the best decision he ever made." He eyed the others, fully aware that he had just cast a long shadow of distrust. Pep's quills pricked up.

Chip the Cheetah, as swift a thinker as he was a runner, sprung into action, "Like Sarah, I'm getting lots of questions about the New Land. Most of our ancestors who lived there have either died or have fading memories. May I suggest that a small group of us inspect the land? I suggest three of our faster members, carrying a few of the smaller ones on our backs. We have a brief weather window before the rains begin so we should leave tomorrow." Eyebrows were raised, and heads began to nod in agreement.

Chip recalled the bell curve lesson from their first meeting. He had already identified the gazelle as a fellow early adopter to change, and the hyena and porcupine at the opposite end, as resisters. Slyly winking at Joy, Chip continued, "I propose that

JayEll the Gazelle accompany me, along with Harry the Hyena." There were a few audible gasps as Harry looked up abruptly, very surprised to hear his name. "The three of us are fast travelers, and can handle the treacherous Great Divide. We can carry Pep and Sarah on our backs, and any other smaller residents who might want to go."

Kat looked up from her notepad, wondering if she would be allowed to make the journey. She was swift, and could bring back photographs to share. Her thoughts were interrupted by Bryce the Bushback, who wisely asserted, "It seems that at least one participant of the Pilot Project should go with you. Since Ross the Rhino and I are slow movers, we will not be able to make the trip. But perhaps Ben the Beetle could hitch a ride with you. His youthful insights may prove to be quite valuable." Ben beamed and said he'd be happy to join the travelers.

Joy smiled, pleased that the careful selection of change agents was already paying off. Not only had the members themselves proposed a viable solution to lingering questions, but they had self-organized a fair representation of members to obtain answers to their questions.

"Excellent! You can all report back to us at next week's meeting. Then we'll put together a list of Frequently Asked Questions, and will include the answers to your questions about the New Land, as well as other topics." Turning to Kat, she said, "It would be great if your editor would allow you and your camera to make the journey. As we all know, a picture is worth 10,000 words!" Kat nodded with excitement.

After entertaining a few more questions, Joy focused the group on a brainstorming exercise for naming their committee and the Change Management process. She explained that it would be important to brand the effort so that communications related to the relocation would be obvious and important. She asked for them to call out their ideas as she listed them on a flipchart. Some were too silly. Some were too serious. Some were boring. Then JayEll rose to his feet and gracefully announced, "EastBound." He even held up a sketch of a possible logo, showing a compass with the needle pointing to the East.

"That's it!" they all cried out in unison.

JayEll asked Pep the Porcupine to take a bow. "Pep is the one who sketched the compass with his sharpest quill. Until he did that, I wasn't sure that 'EastBound' would work. But wow, what a difference a name with a good logo makes!" Pep's quills were laying softly as he looked around and realized that he had indeed contributed in a meaningful way.

"Why that's the fastest I've seen any group select a name and logo! You are all to be commended," said Joy. "You are now called the 'EastBounders' and our Change Management Program will be referenced simply as 'EastBound.' Let's meet here again in one week. Be prepared to learn about the New Land from your scouting party. We will also have two guest speakers, John Jay and Perry, to share with you the preliminary designs for the Pilot Project and the New Land, so be prepared for a longer meeting. Both primary and alternate members should plan to attend." She dismissed them, noting that Kat was already sprinting across the savanna to speak with her editor.

~~~~~~~~~~

Chip and JayEll were deep in conversation on their way back from the journey across the Great Divide. All in all, the trip had gone fine. The group of six had bonded quite nicely during their journey, and didn't mind having Kat along to record their discoveries.

Of course, there had been some tense moments, especially upon arrival when Harry and Pep began a downward spiral of complaints about the loss of enclosed personal space and reduced size of individual habitats. Chip countered by pointing out a few of the unique features that were not presently in their Kingdom, so that had eased their pain a bit. Ben seemed to go with the flow, representative of his younger and carefree generation. But he did pause frequently to ask Kat to take photographs of features that he knew his EastBound Pilot comrades would want to see.

On the way home, Sarah the Shrew surprised everyone by announcing that she wanted to be more mobile in the New Land, without a permanent assigned residence. "Why would anyone

want to settle down in one place when there is so much to see and experience in our New Land?" she challenged. JayEll found himself agreeing with her, and Ben as well. Kat made notes and snapped more photos.

It began to rain as they reached the edge of the Kingdom, where they were met by Joy and the five members of the Guiding Coalition. All were anxious to learn about their journey. Maggie was especially concerned about controlling communications, since Hal had just reported that productivity had returned to normal, and they could not risk rumors spreading like before.

Finding a cave nearby, the scouting party sought shelter out of the rain in which to debrief the EastBound leaders. Kat sat off to the side, respecting Maggie's assertion that the ensuing conversation would be "off the record."

Joy asked each member of the scouting party to candidly share their personal insights, without regard for political correctness. One by one, they shared the plusses and the minuses. When appropriate, Kat supported their statements with photo images stored in her camera. The Guiding Coalition appreciated the direct feedback. All in all, it seemed that the trip was well worth the effort. Honest answers would be provided to the residents, and the EastBounders would need to decide how to handle the hot issues. Furthermore, the scouting party might be able to influence the EastBound Pilot design so that it truly would test key change concepts.

As the rains began to subside, Maggie could sense that the travelers were ready to return home. She flew to a high ledge in the cave and chirped, "Thank you for your honest and direct communications. We look forward to you reporting to the EastBounders tomorrow. In the meantime, we know you will be approached by many friends and family members to comment on the New Land. We ask that you simply say that you look forward to sharing first with the EastBounders. Even if pressed, we ask you not to give any details. It is important that the EastBounders draft answers to the Frequently Asked Questions together. Then we can refer all the residents there. We can use Kat's EastBound column in *The Sun* to share photos, as well as dispatch deputy magpies to deliver FAQ parchments to each village. Make sense?"

The scouts nodded, relieved that Maggie had anticipated their individual dilemmas and given clear instruction for them to follow. As the summer rain ceased, they left the cave and disbanded to return to their respective homes.

~~~~~~~~~~

The grassy knoll at the edge of Kings Park was packed as all thirty -six EastBounders squeezed in, anxious to hear reports from the scouting party. The two designers, John Jay and Perry, had arrived early so they could hear comments from the scouts, which could influence their design ideas. Maggie was in attendance to coordinate follow-up communications. Joy didn't waste any time calling the meeting to order and asking each of the six scouts to make their reports.

JayEll was the first to speak. In vivid detail, he described the New Land's unique features, including the waterfall and large lake as well as the open range bordered by hectares of wildflowers. The EastBounders listened patiently, taking it all in.

Pep the Porcupine went next, and was joined immediately by Harry the Hyena. While most of the Kingdom respected Pep and his practical nature, Harry was not so well-liked due to his often misplaced humor and negative attitude. As difficult as it was to listen to the challenging features of the New Land, the EastBounders clearly appreciated hearing their uncensored report.

Alma the Aardvark nosed her way to the front. "What can you tell us about the accommodations for us nocturnal creatures? It's bad enough that I have to endure these daytime meetings! Once we move, I need to be assured I'll be able to dig my cave, which I can't do near water or rock."

Her question began a frenzy of chatter and inquiry, until Joy rapped on a nearby tree and asked that everyone hold their questions until the last scouting report. Alma crept back to sit near Maggie, hoping her old friend would whisper a few comforting insights during the meeting. But Maggie showed no sign of tipping her wing.

Chip rose to his haunches, quieting the crowd. He spoke of the bonding that occurred among their diverse team of six during the journey. Harry and Pep even nodded in agreement. Chip described the new behaviors that would be necessary and, in fact, welcomed in the New Land, with the mighty and small living in closer proximity to one another. He then invited Ben and Sarah to share their personal insights.

Ben the Beetle spoke first, and was quite nonchalant. He explained that although the New Land was very different, he did not find anything that represented a huge concern to him. He mentioned that Kat would be sharing photos in *The Sun*, and the residents could decide for themselves. "In fact, I sincerely believe that many of you will enjoy this new landscape better than our present Kingdom. Sarah made a bold announcement yesterday on our journey back, and I have to say I plan to join her. Sarah, ready to share your thoughts?"

Sarah looked into the eyes of her fellow EastBounders. "This trip changed me. I now see our New Land as a landscape of opportunity. There is so much to explore, and so many wonderful opportunities. Sure the total area is smaller, but when I think of the advantages of co-location and sharing of resources, I frankly wonder why it took a move to get us to pull together and unify. In fact, I'm so jazzed about the possibilities that I plan to be more mobile in the New Land, without a permanently assigned residence."

As the crowd murmured, gasped, and whispered, JayEll joined Sarah and Ben and said, "To reinforce what Sarah just said, allow me to restate her question posed during our journey yesterday: 'Why would anyone want to settle down in one place when there is so much to see and experience in our New Land?' I have to tell you that she opened my eyes to that possibility, so I too am joining Ben and Sarah as nomads." The murmurs grew louder, and Joy rapped for silence.

JayEll continued, "Please understand that we are not suggesting that our entire Kingdom become nomadic. All we are saying is that the options in our New Land are plentiful, and it's up to each of us to decide how we can live and work optimally in this new landscape. For the three of us, we will be mobile. And we simply want you to know that is but one of many options." The EastBounders quieted down as JayEll took his seat.

Joy thanked the scouts for their reports and nodded to Kat who had just arrived breathless at the edge of the knoll. She distributed a special edition of *The Sun* featuring photos of the New Land. The residents eagerly turned the pages, pointing and whispering. Joy gave them a few minutes, and then asked for questions. For the next half hour, the scouts answered as many questions as they could. Some topics were listed on a flipchart for follow-up later by Joy and the Guiding Coalition. Other topics were listed for the EastBounders to resolve in subsequent meetings. Kat took notes, while John Jay and Perry conferred quietly in preparation for their design presentation. At last, no questions remained, and Joy invited the two designers to address the crowd.

John Jay the Butterfly began by thanking the scouts and acknowledging that their reports would certainly provide added detail to the preliminary design of the Pilot Project. Perry the Zebra echoed similar sentiments for the design development of the New Land.

Then the butterfly explained the purpose of the Pilot Project, what they hoped to learn, the number of participants from the three provinces, and the fast-track schedule. He then took a deep breath and announced the location of the Pilot Project. As expected, the EastBounders' reactions were similar to Lord Badger's and the King's, expressing grave concerns about losing half of Central Park. John Jay was prepared for this and spoke up.

"As you know, I was born and raised in Central Park. I have lived there all my life, and have raised my own young ones there. You couldn't have the Park in better wings than mine for the remaining time in our Kingdom. I commit to you that I will make this Pilot work, and we will still enjoy half of the Park for our sports and other activities," John Jay stated with conviction as the objections faded.

Continuing, John Jay unrolled preliminary plans of the Pilot and proceeded to describe the phased renovations, including the four primary cultural changes to be tested. Looking up at Ben, he said, "Sounds like you'll be helping us test the nomadic lifestyle. We'd like to recruit about twenty percent of the pilot participants to participate." Ben nodded, and began to think of others he could get to join him.

Whitney the Wildebeest arrived in time to give an overview of the detailed schedule, including how games would be relocated to the other half of Central Park, as well as neighboring territories if necessary. He reiterated the importance of beginning the Pilot immediately to test options and ideas.

"We plan to survey the Pilot participants concerning pre-move topics and questions," John Jay continued. "Furthermore, we hope all residents of the Kingdom will take the opportunity to tour the Pilot, and answer a questionnaire about key ideas and design concepts we will be testing. We expect you, as EastBounders, to emphasize to your tribe members the importance of this feedback, and how it shapes our ultimate success." He nodded to Perry, who approached with plans of the New Land.

Perry picked up seamlessly where the butterfly left off. "As John Jay has explained, the Pilot Project will simulate as closely as possible the opportunities and challenges we will face when we move east, especially those related to the four primary cultural changes. The six scouts have provided key insights that I'll be sure to address in future design enhancements. But for now, allow me to share with you the preliminary design concepts."

She unrolled a very long colorful parchment, asking John Jay and Maggie to hold so that all could see. The EastBounders gathered close as Perry shared the key design characteristics of the New Land. Joy marveled at how far Perry had come since presenting to the King last week. Everything was so well organized, and yet organic. Districts, nodes, pathways, edges, and landmarks easily accommodated their population densities. Perry reinforced the scout's report of natural elements that were added benefits of the New Land. She was also careful to mention necessary survival strategies for the Kingdom's mighty and small, such as areas of prospect and refuge. She even noted features that would accommodate nocturnal creatures, earning a slow smile from Alma the Aardvark. Satisfied that she had touched on all the key points, Perry paused to ask for questions.

"Hip Hip Hooray!" exclaimed a hippopotamus from the back of the pack.

"Well done Perry!" added a high-spirited monkey, swinging from a tree limb.

"Tee-hee-hee," laughed Harry the Hyena, as all eyes turned. Perry looked up with curiosity, waiting for him to elaborate. Harry smirked, enjoying the attention. He then knitted his brows into a serious face, and asked a few questions about privacy challenges in densely populated areas. Perry acknowledged that she had more work to do regarding that concept and invited him as well as others to a design workshop the following day. Several eager paws and legs were raised, including Alma's. After a few more minutes of questioning, Perry rolled up the parchment after allowing Kat to snap a few photos for the EastBound column.

Joy thanked both designers and announced that the next meeting would be a true work session, with EastBounders divvying up list of flipchart questions and seeking answers. Meanwhile, Maggie would be summarizing the questions they could answer immediately, and would be dispatching deputy magpies to deliver FAQ parchments to the tribes. EastBounders were reminded to act as liaisons, communicating to their tribes all the important information they had just received.

~~~~~~~~~~~~

The next weeks flew by. EastBound was on the tip of the tongues of the mighty and small. No resident was overlooked. Not only did Kat's column appear in every habitat, but Maggie made sure that her deputy magpies delivered special messages on parchments when necessary. The EastBound change agents continued to meet and were constantly dreaming up new activities and events to further communicate upcoming changes. Each EastBounder had volunteered to either lead or join a sub-committee, according to their skillset and interest.

Of particular note was Ross the Rhino. Ross was doing an outstanding job heading the "No Hoarding" committee, using the Pilot participants as a beta test group. Their charge was to transition residents from hoarding to sharing, and this was proving to be quite the challenge. But Ross was creative, and constantly on the lookout for innovative ideas. He knew that reducing hoarding was one of the five key Change Management goals, and he understood that the success of the Pilot group was important to their success in the New Land.

Likewise, JayEll had volunteered to lead a subset in developing the Kingdom Etiquette Guidelines to leverage their physical space for the greater good. JayEll had a team of seven drafting and honing the etiquette guidelines that would help to shape desired animal behaviors. They were currently testing the guidelines among the Pilot Participants, and were encouraged with the outcomes thus far.

Hoping to involve more residents in communications, Maggie encouraged another EastBounder to lead special projects. Anne the Ant, queen of her colony and a highly respected taskmaster, was skilled at managing concurrent projects. She was assisted by Jill the Jackal, a member of the Pilot Project. This dynamic duo recruited numerous residents to work on projects that required very little time, but engaged them in fun activities heightening awareness of the impending move such as purge campaigns, scavenger hunts, focus groups, trivia contests, and welcome packages. Bryce the Bushback had suggested burying time capsules in each of the Provinces, so Anne and Jill had asked

each tribe to gather one item to place in the capsules upon their departure.

After the sixth week of the Pilot Project occupancy, Joy asked to meet with Lady K to review overall progress regarding the eight steps of change. "Lady K, EastBound appears to be a success and I am intent on sustaining our momentum. I believe that steps four and five, Communicate Change Vision and Empower Broad-Based Action, are firmly in place. Last month's scouting party not only empowered an important subset of the EastBounders, but the trip certainly achieved step six, Generate Short-Term Wins, as did that recent article in *The Sun* highlighting how design decisions have been influenced by the scouting reports and the pre-move survey. It was interesting to read the interview with Harry the Hyena --- he has certainly toned down his early resistance!" Lady K nodded her head in agreement.

"With the Pilot participants fully settled into their new lifestyles," Joy continued, "I am keenly aware that we have a unique opportunity to achieve step seven, Consolidate and Build on Gains. It's been enough time, and there have been plenty of initiatives, to celebrate the successes of the Pilot Project. I propose that the King host a Kingdom-wide party at Central Park, to recognize the contributions of the Pilot participants, while highlighting the many ways that their efforts have informed our relocation plans."

Lady K hopped with excitement. "Excellent idea my friend! And do you realize we are at the halfway point? We move in just three months! This event will emphasize the need to keep the momentum going. I have a meeting this evening with the other members of the Guiding Coalition. I will bring this up, and will schedule a meeting with the King if they concur."

~~~~~~~~~~

Lights sparkled and fireworks lit the dark skies. All of the Kingdom had gathered in Central Park for the "Halfway to EastBound" Celebration. Even the nocturnal creatures were celebrating, despite disruption to their normal activities. The King had just honored each of the Pilot participants with purple glow sticks around their necks, and had roared a proclamation listing their accomplishments. The King also recognized the EastBounders with orange glow sticks, called out the scouting party by name, and thanked them all for their hard work. The Guiding Coalition and Joy looked over the merry crowd and knew that they had come a long way in a short period of time. They still had much to accomplish, but for now, it was the time to celebrate.

The next morning, Joy convened a meeting of the EastBounders. She had invited Hal and Maggie to attend as well to listen for operational and communication strategies as appropriate. They gathered on the western edge of Central Park, while clean-up crews worked around them. It was obvious that it had been an evening of merriment and celebration. Many were still sporting their glowing necklaces that were slowly fading in the sunlight.

"EastBounders, you are to be commended for all of your hard work," Joy began. "With your help, the Pilot Project has been a success. We have learned much, and that knowledge has influenced Perry's final designs. Wasn't it wonderful to hear the King roar that proclamation last night?!"

Harry snickered and said, "Actually, it was more fun watching Pep dancing with the Dowager!"

Joy smiled, and continued. "Today, we need to fully grasp that we have just three months before the move. It is imperative that we build on the wins of our efforts to date. And it's time to plan how we will Anchor New Approaches in the New Land, which is step eight of creating change. Let's hear report-outs from each of our sub-committees on their efforts to date, and their plans moving forward. JayEll, I'd like to begin with you. Your work developing etiquette guidelines is a critical component in achieving step eight."

One by one, each of the EastBounders summarized what they had been doing, what seemed to be sticking, and where they still needed assistance. Ross reported that the initial resistance of the Pilot participants to the "no hoarding" policy was overcome through strategically encouraged peer pressure. JayEll took note, hoping that peer pressure would also help enforce the etiquette guidelines after the move to the New Land. Anne the Ant summarized the many smaller projects that had engaged a broad representation of residents, leading to unity and happiness, which was one of the five Change Management goals.

Satisfied that they were on the right track, Joy invited Hal and Maggie to provide operational and communication updates. As Maggie wrapped up with a summary tweet, the sky suddenly darkened and the air grew still. All paused, looking up and around. They knew what this meant.

With a strong gust from the north, the winds changed direction. They blew fast and hard, punctuated with strong gusts that flattened Maggie's feathers and Pep's quills in an instant. They all huddled together, bracing themselves against the northern wind, and moved en masse toward the shelter of a nearby cave.

Suddenly, they were aware of fiercely pounding hooves. All eyes turned east to see Whitney battling the wind to join them. As he approached, the intensity of his eyes told them what they already knew.

"EastBounders, the north winds have arrived, one month ahead of schedule," the wildebeest announced. "This has serious implications for our move. According to my calculations we now have just two months before the rains begin. I am on my way to the King's lair to advise him that we must be prepared to move one month earlier in order to safely cross the Great Divide."

With a renewed sense of urgency, Whitney unrolled his detailed schedule and the EastBounders gathered around, understanding where they would need to tighten up their plans. Maggie fiercely took notes, regretting that Kat was not in attendance. Hal altered efficiency goals to reflect an earlier move schedule, though less concerned since Ross had made significant progress on the "no hoarding" policies.

By the time Whitney bounded out of the cave towards the King's lair, the north wind had settled to a consistent breeze, and the sun was shining again. Joy addressed the EastBounders, "This indeed changes our plans. But to be honest, we are extremely prepared. Because you took your responsibilities seriously, and worked early to begin to implement changes, this earlier move date is achievable. You each know what you need to do now. So let's get busy!"

Turning to the Maggie, Joy added, "We will count on you to update all the residents, even though the changing winds should have tipped them off. We can't take anything for granted. Time is of the essence." And with that, she dismissed the EastBounders who scattered to fast-track their plans.

~~~~~~~~~~

Two months flew by, with the north winds a constant reminder that change was coming. Perry worked with Whitney to assure that the designs for the New Land would be ready. Hal requested assistance from the EastBounders to appoint move coordinators within each of the tribes to oversee all move related concerns, which helped to keep productivity high during the last weeks. Maggie coordinated seamless communications with Kat and the deputy magpies, who used The Philippe Meister's carrier pigeons when necessary. The EastBounders found it necessary to involve additional residents in the work due to a compressed schedule, which unified the Kingdom even more.

The day before the move, the King invited the mighty and small to join him in Central Park to pay tribute to their prized savanna during a festive carnival-like celebration. Anne the Ant had scheduled several large group events featuring speakers from The Guiding Coalition. She also assigned smaller booths staffed by EastBounders, a few Pilot Participants, and the two designers, so that residents could get answers to any remaining questions. Joy was amused to see that Harry and Pep were staffing a booth called "Change is Hard" and had a pawful of residents in line who were bending their ears on lingering concerns. She noted with relief that their booth had the smallest line.

As the sun began its descent, the King climbed to the highest rock in Central Park. A hush fell over the Kingdom as the King addressed the crowds. "Five months ago, I instilled a sense of urgency by announcing that our land is being threatened and our Kingdom must relocate. I placed our future in the hands of the Guiding Coalition, who outlined a compelling vision and strategy. Rather than executing that strategy on their own, they engaged each and every one of you, fully understanding that our Bold Cultural Change would only be embraced if it was implemented bottom up as well as top down. Through internal and external communication methods, each of you received timely news and information about our relocation, branded EastBound. A special group of change agents was formed to help empower broad-based action, and we all have appreciated their diligent work." The King paused, and asked the EastBounders to be recognized while the crowd expressed their gratitude.

Lady K and Joy locked eyes, realizing that the King was subtly outlining the eight steps to change as part of his send-off speech. The King continued, "We also recognize the efforts of the brave scouting party and Pilot Participants. They gave us honesty, and they gave us reasons to believe that this change could in fact be a good thing. And we celebrated their efforts two months ago in this very place." He motioned for the scouting party and Pilot Participants to be recognized. Applause and whistles resounded throughout the park.

The King could sense the growing excitement. "Since then, we have been building on what we learned, and each of you has contributed in ways both great and small. Even when the north winds arrived one month early, you didn't lose your footing. You kept working, knowing how critical it would be to anchor our new behaviors as much as possible in preparation for the move. You put strategies in place to 'make it stick' as we move across the Great Divide. And I have every confidence that we will succeed, because in my opinion, we already have!"

Pandemonium erupted as the mighty and small applauded one another. The King was right. They had already been changed.

The King waited for the crowd to quiet. "Tomorrow brings a new day and a new life. We bury our time capsules to honor our past, for it has been a good journey and a faithful savanna. And we embark on our new journey, unified as a Kingdom in ways none of us could have envisioned a mere year ago. We are as prepared as any Kingdom could be for the Bold Cultural Change that awaits us in the New Land. We depart in hopeful anticipation. We also understand that we may encounter the unexpected, and yet, we know that we will face any challenges together, unified as we are EastBound."

The King nodded to the Philippe Meister who in turn orchestrated hundreds of carrier pigeons to deliver decorated departure packages to each resident. In each package was a map, along a detailed itinerary for the following day. As the residents opened their packages, a rock band in the center of the park struck up their Kingdom anthem which they could hear as they returned to their homes for their final evening in their prized savanna.

~~~~~~~~~~

Joy stood under the EastBound sculpture, a noticeable landmark in the middle of the largest wildflower patch in the New Land, edged by a small grove of trees. The winds were blowing softly from the East as the EastBounders crossed the plain towards her. Kat sprinted ahead of them, intent on photographing another historic occasion. It was hard to believe it had already been four months since their journey across the Great Divide.

"Thank you for joining me for our last official meeting as EastBounders," Joy began. "Our work is nearly completed as the appointed change agents for our relocation. I'd like to begin with the results of our post-move survey, and then hear from JayEll on the implementation of the etiquette guidelines. Sarah, perhaps you can fill us in on the concerns raised by your fellow nomads last week? Does anyone else have anything to report?"

"We'd like to have a final word, if that's okay," said Lady K from the shade of a nearby tree. Joy looked up and smiled to see all the members of the Guiding Coalition.

"Certainly," said Joy. "Come join us to hear the reports."

Chip reviewed the results of the survey, beginning with a reminder. "You will recall that the post-move survey was purposefully distributed three months after our relocation, in order to give us time to settle into our new habitats. Even though JayEll's team reviewed the etiquette guidelines with all the tribes in the months prior to our move, we knew it would take some time for new habits to form and new behaviors to take hold."

"You can say that again," muttered Harry a bit too loudly. He looked around, surprised to see several of the EastBounders agreeing with him.

Chip presented summary results of the post-move survey,

including a few themes that dominated the responses to the open-ended questions. Hal made a note to obtain the full report from Chip later, since he suspected productivity could be increased with further understanding of key issues. All in all, the residents were settling in quite well. Chip reported that seventy-two percent said they would not want to return to their prior land. Of those that were Pilot Participants, the percentage was even higher, at ninety-five percent.

"That's remarkable!" marveled Pep the Porcupine. "And we've only been here a few months. The Pilot group had a good head start. I suspect those numbers will increase as our habits and behaviors continue to develop. I know I've adjusted a bit more since answering that survey."

Chip nodded, quoting a few responses submitted in the open-ended questions. "The tighter boundaries have brought us together more as a community... Perry's use of edges and nodes has really helped define our tribunal district in what would have otherwise been a wide open field... Our 'no hoarding' policy has helped me learn to live in a space that is half the size of my former habitat... At first I thought the etiquette guidelines were common sense, but more than once I've had to refer my noisy neighbor to the guidelines, and that usually resolves our issue."

Chip paused to answer a few questions and then gave a nod to JayEll to brief everyone on peer enforcement of the etiquette guidelines, which was apparently going well. Sarah reported on the resolution of issues raised by several of the nomad newbies, which again were resolved by peer groups. Members of the Guiding Coalition were especially pleased to hear how conflicts were being resolved by the residents themselves, rather than ending up in their laps.

Joy lifted her long neck and could see that their work had drawn to a beautiful close. "EastBounders, you have faithfully executed what we set out to do nine months ago. It has been my honor to lead this change with you. Let's turn our attention to the Guiding Coalition for their parting words."

Lady K approached, hopping onto a rock under the sculpture, so that she could make eye contact with each member of the EastBounders, mighty and small. Lord Badger and the Dowager were at her side, while Hal and Maggie flew to the top of the sculpture. Lady K paused before she spoke, reflecting on the events that had led them to this place.

Lady K began, "EastBounders, you have dutifully fulfilled your responsibilities as change agents for the King. I hope you realize that you are largely responsible for the ease of transition our residents have experienced.

"You worked hard to help us meet our five Change Management goals. Because of your efforts, we achieved every one, the most important of which was 'unified and happy residents.' The Dowager, Lord Badger, and I thank you for the unity you have

Change is on the Wind

106

brought to each of our provinces. Hal thanks you for keeping productivity high, even in the midst of extreme change. And Maggie thanks you for being the primary communication link, putting a face on the real messages of change to those you represented." Lady K paused as Lord Badger led them in a round of applause, while the Dowager handed out wildflower bouquets to each of the EastBound members. She saved the largest bouquet for Joy the Giraffe, who beamed her appreciation.

The breeze picked up as Lady K offered her parting words. "We look forward to your continued leadership as residents in this Land of Bold Cultural Change. Together, we will always be EastBound." As they departed, the winds carried the roar of approval from the King's small yet ample lair, high on a rocky ledge on the eastern edge of the New Land.

Endnotes

[1] John Seely Brown, Stephen Denning, Katalina Groh, & Laurence Prusak (2004). *Storytelling in Organizations, Why Storytelling Is Transforming 21st Century Organizations and Management*. New York, NY. Routledge.

[2] Frank Duffy, architect, is often quoted to say: "As architects, we prepare space for the people. As change managers, we prepare people for the space."

[3] John P. Kotter (1996). *Leading Change*. Harvard, MA. Harvard Business School Press. Also, visit his website, http://www.kotterinternational.com/our-principles/changesteps

[4] quotation adapted from James Belasco and Ralph Stayer (1994). *Flight of the Buffalo: Soaring to Excellence, Learning to Let Employees Lead*. New York, NY. Warner Books, Inc.

Summary of Key Ideas

It is worth noting a few key ideas conveyed within the fable.

New construction or renovation projects offer unique opportunities for change. Quite often, bold cultural changes result and the intended occupants of these new spaces require support to fully embrace these changes. An effective Change Management program parallels the design and construction process, and ensures that occupants will be prepared for the new space and immediately productive after the move.

If you are a corporate executive, facility manager, real estate advisor, interior designer, architect, urban planner, human resource director, organization development practitioner, or program manager, this book was written for you. You may already recognize several portions in the story as key factors that would "make or break" the success of a relocation or new construction project. An effective Change Management program will address these critical components.

Part One

News of the Change

- The four key cultural changes in this fable are frequently the leading challenges caused by shrinking real estate. Facility managers are expected to implement these or similar new workplace strategies, and must determine if a Change Management program would help ensure success.

- If the key cultural changes for an organization are not recognized, communicated, and accepted, serious consequences may result, including loss of key personnel, internal rebellions, disenfranchised staff, and loss of productivity.

- CEOs often rely upon advisors who may not all be equal in their communication skills, scope of influence, length of service, intrinsic motivation, or readiness for change. These emergent characteristics become critical factors that must be recognized and addressed for ultimate success.

- CEOs often confide early with a few senior leaders, sharing in-depth detail about the reasons behind a future move. However, when eventually delivering an announcement to an assembly of employees, whether verbal or written, pertinent details may wind-up being omitted from the CEO's message, resulting in the spread of misinformation, which in turn results in lost productivity and loss of trust. To avoid this, communications managers should be involved early and often to advise senior leadership, with intentional consideration of staff perspective.

- It is critical that departmental or senior leaders be advised on what, and when, to share information with their staff. Some leaders share more openly, while others hold information close. This inequity can quickly fuel the rumor mill, resulting in productivity loss and wild speculation that may inflict internal damage as well as compromise external relations.

- John P. Kotter's "Eight Steps to Creating Change" (as outlined in *Leading Change* and several of his other books) provide an excellent framework that can be easily adapted and fully integrated into change management programs.

Part Two

The Hard Work of Change

- It is often necessary to "make a case" for implementing a Change Management program. The four components outlined in the fable are essential in convincing others that Change Management is a wise investment. Human Resource metrics can often provide compelling numbers to support Change Management, e.g., costs to replace one valuable employee who resigns due to relocation.

- It is imperative to have a clear vision and strategy for Change Management. It keeps everyone focused. At times, issues arise midway through the project, and it may not be clear whether the issue is a Change Management concern or resides elsewhere in the organization. A quick check against the Change Management goals will help to clarify.

- It is helpful to have a mix of early adopters as well as

resisters in advisory roles. If resisters can be converted or placated, others will begin to believe that change can be embraced.

- Change Agent Committees are ideally twelve to eighteen members, with assigned alternates to assure consistency. Diversity is key, across a broad spectrum, to include age, gender, race, functional position, longevity with the organization, and readiness for change. The member's primary function is to represent their department/ division and act as a communications liaison. Meeting frequency depends on the demands of the project, but typically is most frequent at the launch, then again just prior to the move.

- The Change Agent Committee should be involved in brainstorming activities that appropriately parallel the design and construction schedule. This keeps the process relevant as well as interesting.

- The selection of someone to lead the Change Management program is critical. This facilitator must have exceptional communication skills and task management abilities. The position may be filled internally or externally, as long as the primary job responsibility is Change Management.

- It is imperative to outline clear Change Management

goals in support of the broader project goals. They are related, but distinct.

- The Change Management facilitator must stay in close contact with design and communication team members, and should regularly seek input from human resources, facilities, and technology leaders.

- Not all new construction or renovation projects have time or space to pilot new concepts as described in the fable. However, most projects can at least include mock-ups of furniture and/or architectural features in order to gather feedback prior to specification and order placement. Even mock-ups composed of foam core board or cardboard can communicate spatial ideas that can be quite valuable when testing new concepts.

Part Three

Preparing Others for the Change

- It is critical to have senior leadership visibly and vocally endorse the Change Management program throughout the project duration.

- It is important to brand the Change Management effort with a name and a logo, including the Change Agent Committee.

- Field trips to similar project types, as well as hard hat tours, are very effective ways to gather important information and communicate design concepts.

- Step five, Empower Broad-Based Action, is a critical component of success. Change Agent Committees become the leading instruments of change in both public and private sector organizations. Their participation, especially in pilot projects or mock-up reviews, also provides results that assist with step six, Generate Short Term Wins.

- With any relocation or renovation, it is important to discover and communicate the benefits and the "good news" while honestly describing the intended changes, many of which may be initially perceived as negative. Quite often, once the initial shock has dissipated, staff will begin to understand and accept the reasons for the change, especially if involved in the Change Management process.

- Pre-Move surveys are effective in identifying key "hot-buttons" for the staff, and alerting leadership to challenges that they may not have expected. When uncovered early in the process, solutions can be pursued for optimal resolution, often avoiding costly changes after occupancy.

- Post-Move surveys should be conducted at least three to six months after occupancy to allow for new habits to form and occupants to settle into their new space and routines. Similarly, a moratorium on change should be adhered to for at least three months for the same reasons.

- It is important to communicate examples of how the Change Agent Committee or other staff members may influence the design, in ways great or small.

- Design workshops and focus groups are great methods to resolve conflict while including a larger representation of all staff.

- It is imperative to use many and various methods of multi -media communications to reach the most people.

- Workplace etiquette guidelines, developed by the Change Agent Committee, can be extremely effective in communicating and enforcing desired behavioral changes.

- Celebration events should be planned occasionally throughout the project, marking significant milestones. It is also important to honor the past, giving recognition to historical achievements. Leaders should be present at these events to offer recognition and thanks.

Acknowledgments

There are many people and organizations who inspired me to write this book, and who supported me on this journey.

First and foremost, I thank my customers, who have entrusted me to lead their Change Management programs. We have explored and navigated these uncharted waters together, since Change Management is a new and emerging discipline in workplace design. I am especially grateful to Howard County Government in the State of Maryland, who has retained my Change Management services for three distinct projects, and now lists Change Management as a required discipline in their RFP process. There is no greater affirmation for the value that these services have provided.

Thank you to my professors and classmates at the Weatherhead School of Management at Case Western Reserve University. When I enrolled to pursue a Master's in Positive Organization Development and Change (MPOD), I did so with the intent to enhance and elevate my interior design consulting practice. The education and experience I received with my MPOD degree fulfilled my dream to link organization development with workplace design, and provided a strong foundation to design and hone a change management process that truly works.

Thank you to the International Facility Management Association, who provided my "sense of urgency" to write about change management in support of two conference presentations.

Thank you to my illustrator, the talented Caroline Devereaux, who brought these characters to life beyond what I had imagined.

Thank you to my two editors, Buzz Bartlett and Sarah Wortman, who both responded with valuable insights and spot-on edits despite tight deadlines.

Thank you to my niece, Amy Miller, who introduced me to Craig Schenning, a caring and responsive publisher.

To my inspirational parents, Margaret and Pep Pepmeier, the ultimate change managers: Thank you for always believing in me and supporting my dreams, even if you weren't quite sure where they would lead. No words can adequately express my appreciation for your wisdom and abiding love.

To my stepdaughter Kathryn: Thank you for bringing your positive glow and adventuresome spirit into our family, and for supporting your dad and me in the pursuit of our dreams.

To my sons, Philippe and Jean-Luc: Thank you for your unwavering trust through all the many changes the three of us have weathered together. You have always supported and encouraged me in my professional and personal pursuits, and I hope to always convey the same to you with similar grace and understanding.

And finally, to my husband Dudley Whitney, my amazing partner in business and in life: Thank you for supporting this endeavor with your wise counsel, patient ear, and tireless editing. Your keen insights gleaned from facilitating change management programs with me added clarity to the story. It is truly a pleasure to sail the journey of life with you, and I look forward to open waters very soon. I promise.

About the Author

Cheryl Duvall is a consultant, designer, speaker, coach, writer, and entrepreneur. She founded Avancé in recognition of her passion for interior design and the important role it plays in shaping behaviors in the workplace.

Cheryl enjoys leading strategic planning efforts that explore alternative approaches to the design of the office environment. She uses creative change management techniques to engage building occupants throughout the design process, thus increasing their acceptance of change within the workplace.

Cheryl holds a M.S. in Positive Organization Development and Change from Case Western Reserve University, and a B.S. in Interior Design from University of Maryland. She has been responsible for the design of eleven million square feet of interiors in addition to more than a dozen change initiatives. Her clients include Cisco Systems, Herman Miller, Virginia Department of Transportation, and HanesBrands.

She is a past President of the International Interior Design

Association, and was inducted into its College of Fellows in 1993. Cheryl is a noted writer, having served as Executive Editor of *Perspective* magazine, and is one of several contributing authors to McGraw-Hill's *Interior Design Handbook of Professional Practice*, for which she authored the chapter "Specialty Practices." She is a frequent speaker on various topics, including change management, coworking, innovative officing, and work-life fullness.

Prior to forming Avancé in 2001, Cheryl was Senior Vice President of GHK Associates, a Top 20 interior design firm as ranked annually by *Interior Design* magazine. She led their Baltimore and Washington, D.C. offices after their acquisition of her firm, Duvall/Hendricks, in 1995. When she isn't working, you can find her sailing with her husband on the Chesapeake Bay, and waters beyond.

For more information about Cheryl, or to inquire about her speaking availability and consulting practice, visit www.avancellc.com or email cduvall@avancellc.com.

CPSIA information can be obtained at www.ICGtesting.com
Printed in the USA
BVOW01*1805170215

387592BV00002B/2/P